JOHN GLENN

TOM STREISSGUTH

In Consultation with Martha Cosgrove,
M.A. and Reading Specialist

LERNER PUBLICATIONS COMPANY/MINNEAPOLIS

Martha Cosgrove, a language arts teacher in Minnesota, has a master's degree from the University of Minnesota in secondary education, with an emphasis on developmental and remedial reading. She is licenced in 7–12 English and language arts, developmental reading, and remedial reading. She has had several works published, and she gives numerous state and national presentations in her areas of expertise.

Lerner Publications Company
A division of Lerner Publishing Group
241 First Avenue North
Minneapolis, Minnesota U.S.A.

Website address: www.lernerbooks.com

Library of Congress Cataloging-in-Publication Data

Streissguth, Thomas, 1958–
   John Glenn / by Tom Streissguth.
       p.   cm. – (Just the facts biographies)
   Includes bibliographical references and index.
   ISBN: 0–8225–2274–8 (lib. bdg. : alk. paper)
   1. Glenn, John, 1921– –Juvenile literature. 2. Legislators–United States–
Biography–Juvenile literature. 3. United States. Congress. Senate–
Biography–Juvenile literature. 4. Astronauts–United States–Biography–
Juvenile literature. I. Title. II. Series.
   E840.8.G54S77 2005
   973.92'092–dc22   2004002617

Manufactured in the United States of America
1 2 3 4 5 6 – JR – 10 09 08 07 06 05

Contents

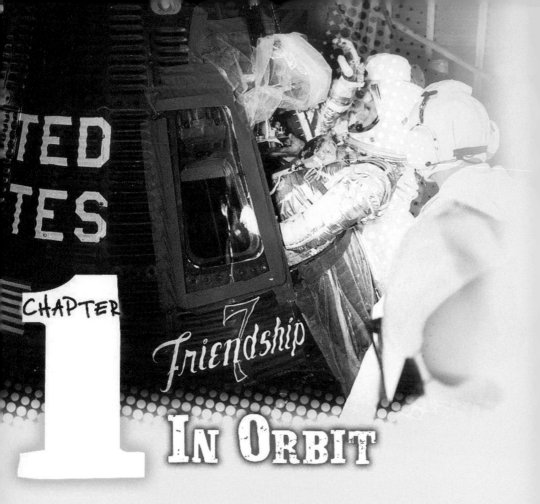

1 IN ORBIT

Friendship 7

TED
TES

(Above)
**John Glenn
is helped
into the
spacecraft
Friendship 7
just before
liftoff in
February
1962.**

AFTER SEVERAL disappointing delays, John Glenn prepared for his first flight into space. His mission would be the third crewed space flight by the United States. Alan Shepard had been the first American to go into space. Gus Grissom had been the second. No American had yet orbited Earth.

Glenn's spacecraft, *Friendship 7,* lifted off from Cape Canaveral in Florida on February 20,

1962. Millions of people watched on television as an Atlas rocket pushed the small, tube-shaped capsule into the sky. The capsule shook as it approached the speed of sound. The speed built up to a force of 6 g's (six times the normal force of gravity on Earth). Glenn's body felt like it weighed a thousand pounds. The weight forced him back into his seat, but his pulse and blood pressure were steady. After reaching a speed of 17,500 miles an hour, the capsule separated from the booster rocket. *Friendship 7*'s altitude was about 550,000 feet. The speed of the craft and Earth's gravity were in balance. This allowed the capsule to reach orbit. Glenn had become the first American to orbit Earth!

The g-forces decreased until Glenn was weightless. Small thrusters turned the capsule to give Glenn a view of Earth, one hundred miles beneath him. Flying backward, he could see dust storms in the Sahara Desert. He saw a huge ring of lights in Perth, Australia. The people of Perth had turned on every light in the city to greet him. "Oh, that view is tremendous!" he exclaimed to the flight engineers on the ground at the National Aeronautics and Space Administration (NASA). It was a feeling Glenn would never forget.

EARLY DAYS

On July 18, 1921, John Hershel Glenn Jr. was born in Cambridge, Ohio. When Glenn was young, his parents moved to the nearby town of New Concord. Both towns lie along the old National Road. Many immigrants in the 1800s had taken this road into the Ohio River Valley and the Midwest. New Concord's founders were Presbyterians—strict religious people who came from England and Scotland. Presbyterians believed in hard work and the importance of family and community. In the 1920s, most people of New Concord still held those beliefs, which also strongly influenced Glenn.

John Glenn's parents stand in front of his boyhood home in New Concord, Ohio.

The Glenn family had a proud military history. Two of John Glenn's great-grandfathers had fought for the North, also called the Union, during the Civil War (1861–1865). Glenn's father had fought in France during World War I (1914–1918). The fighting had damaged his hearing. After the war, John Glenn Sr. came home and started a plumbing business.

John Glenn's mother was Clara Sproat Glenn. She was strong-willed and outgoing. She wanted a large family, but two of her children died when they were babies. After Glenn was born, the family adopted a girl named Jean. Clara told her children that each person is placed on Earth for a purpose. She taught Glenn about the importance of duty.

IT'S A FACT!

John Glenn was named John after his father. His father went by his middle name, Herschel. Glenn's childhood nickname was Bud.

Glenn had a happy childhood and especially enjoyed playing sports such as stickball and hockey. Although he was not a great natural athlete, he always played hard. His parents and teachers could tell that Glenn was a natural leader. For example, New Concord was too small to have its own Boy

Scout troop, so Glenn started his own group, which he called the Ohio Rangers.

GROWING UP

At a young age, Glenn became interested in airplanes and flight. He read books about flying and built wooden models in his room. His hero was Charles Lindbergh. In 1927, when Glenn was almost six, Lindbergh became the first person to fly alone across the Atlantic Ocean. One day, a family friend invited Glenn and his father on a short airplane ride. The flight thrilled the younger Glenn, who decided then

Charles Lindbergh and his plane, the *Spirit of St. Louis*

IT'S A FACT!

The plane Glenn flew in was a Waco biplane. It had an open cockpit, meaning the flyers were open to the air as they flew.

and there that he wanted to be a pilot someday.

In the 1930s, a serious business downturn, called the Great Depression, hit the United States. Many people in New Concord lost their jobs. John Glenn Sr.'s plumbing business also suffered. The Glenn family always had enough to eat, but they saw many others go hungry and lose their homes.

In response to the Depression, U.S. president Franklin D. Roosevelt began programs to help people find work. His actions showed Glenn that politicians could do more than just campaign for election. The Glenn family supported Roosevelt's Democratic Party. Most of the other people in New Concord were Republicans, the other major U.S. political party. So the Glenns were politically out of step with their neighbors.

In 1935, the country began to pull out of the Depression. That year, Glenn entered New Concord High School, where he earned good marks. He worked hard to excel in football, basketball, and

John Glenn was a member of the New Concord Varsity Club. He is in the front row, third from the left.

tennis. Glenn studied American government with a teacher named Harford Steele. Mr. Steele sparked Glenn's interest in American history and the U.S. Congress. Later, Glenn's classmates elected him president of the junior class.

THE COLLEGE YEARS

During high school, Annie Castor, a childhood family friend, caught Glenn's eye, and they became sweethearts. After high school, they both stayed in New Concord to attend Muskingum College. Glenn entered the college in the fall of 1939. Muskingum strictly controlled the behavior of its students. Students couldn't drive cars, smoke, drink, or stay out late. Glenn never had a problem with Muskingum's rules and was a good student. He

IT'S A FACT!

Presbyterians founded Muskingum College in 1837. It was one of the first U.S. colleges that admitted both men and women.

played on the football team and was a member of the Varsity Club, which worked with all of the school's athletic programs.

Life in New Concord was quiet, but trouble was brewing in other parts of the world. These troubles

John Glenn

Annie Castor

Adolf Hitler (standing in car) reviews German troops.

would soon draw in Glenn and other young men and women. Under the leadership of Adolf Hitler, Germany was strengthening its army. This army invaded the countries of Austria and Czechoslovakia in 1938. In 1939 Hitler ordered the invasion of Poland. This action started World War II (1939–1945).

At first, the United States tried to stay out of the war. But some people, including Glenn, believed that the United States would one day enter the war to help U.S. allies such as England and

France. Pilot training programs started throughout the country. Although still in college, Glenn entered a pilot training program at New Philadelphia, a nearby airfield, in 1940. There, he learned the basics of flight, takeoffs, landings, and instrument flying. He completed the program and earned his private pilot's license in July 1941.

Later that year, on December 7, Japan attacked a U.S. naval base at Pearl Harbor on the Hawaiian island of Oahu. Japan was one of Germany's allies. The next day, President

Planes and boats burned after the Japanese attack on Pearl Harbor in December 1941.

Roosevelt declared war on Japan. On December 11, Germany and Italy declared war on the United States. Glenn decided to follow in the footsteps of his father and great-grandfathers by defending his country. It was his chance to show his patriotism and bravery. He dropped out of college and joined the Navy Air Corps. In early 1942, he was sent to a naval air base in Corpus Christi, Texas. Thousands of pilots trained at Corpus Christi before going on active duty. Glenn was eager to start flying for the U.S. Navy.

CHAPTER 2
FIGHTING IN THE AIR

BY THE TIME GLENN WAS training at Corpus Christi, airplanes had become an essential part of every country's military. But the United States didn't yet have a separate air force. Each military branch ran its own air force. The largest was the Army Air Corps. Smaller air forces belonged to the U.S. Navy and the Marine Corps. Each branch of the service also had its own training bases for pilots.

The Corpus Christi Naval Air Station was near the Gulf of Mexico. John Glenn began his military flight training in PBY seaplanes. These small planes can take off and land

> ## IT'S A FACT!
> The "PB" of PBY stands for patrol bomber. "Y" was the manufacturer's code for this version of the plane.

At Corpus Christi, new pilots like Glenn checked boards for last-minute instructions.

on ground or on water. He took classes in navigation and weapons. To practice his skills, he patrolled the Gulf of Mexico to look for enemy submarines.

Glenn earned high marks at Corpus Christi and graduated as a lieutenant. Glenn wasn't sure he wanted a military career. When a Marine Corps recruiter told him that he probably wasn't good enough for the corps, Glenn took it as a challenge and signed up. Soon after getting his flying wings, Glenn married Annie Castor.

FIRST ASSIGNMENTS

Glenn started in the Marine Corps at Cherry Point, North Carolina. He looked forward to training in fighter planes and bombers. But at the time, the Marines had more pilots than planes. Glenn got little flying time. Flight time was very important to military pilots, who needed practice to prepare for real combat.

Glenn was moved from Cherry Point to Camp Kearney, California, where he flew transport planes. He then moved to El Centro Naval Air Facility in California to train in fighter planes. He trained in F4F Wildcats and Corsairs, single-engine planes with a lot of firepower. Glenn was still eager to try out his combat skills.

In February 1944, more than two years after the United States entered the war, Glenn got new orders. The cargo ship *Santa Monica* took him to a base on Midway Island in the Pacific Ocean. This small island is located at the northwestern edge of the Hawaiian Islands. Midway had been the site of a huge naval air battle in 1942. After the United States had won the battle, Japan was no longer a threat to the area. But Japanese ships still lurked in the area, and Glenn's mission was to patrol for Japanese ships, planes, and submarines. That summer, he joined the fighting in the Marshall Islands, located in the central Pacific Ocean. U.S. forces on the ground were suffering

U.S. Marines rest soon after landing on the Marshall Islands in 1944.

heavy losses to the Japanese. U.S. commanders decided to bomb the enemy off the islands, and Glenn flew his Corsair on dozens of successful bombing missions. He was finally in real combat!

To end the war in the Pacific, the United States dropped atomic bombs on the Japanese cities of Hiroshima and Nagasaki on August 6 and August 9, 1945. On August 14, Japan surrendered. The end of the war led Glenn to consider some important decisions. He could retire from the military and return to Annie and his parents in New Concord. Glenn's father wanted to turn over his plumbing business to his son. Glenn also could continue his career as a pilot, either as a commercial airline pilot or as a pilot in the Marine Corps.

FAMILY DECISIONS

Glenn didn't want to leave the excitement of military flying behind him. The Marines still needed pilots to fly new planes. Glenn accepted an offer to stay in the Marine Corps.

The decision wasn't easy. Glenn and Annie had started a family. Their son, David, was born in 1945. On March 15, 1947, Annie gave birth to a daughter named Carolyn, usually called Lyn.

Glenn was stationed in Okinawa, Japan, when Lyn was born. Soon after the birth, Annie suffered an infection and a dangerous fever. Her parents rushed her back to the hospital. When Glenn learned about Annie's fever, he got emergency leave and flew home.

IT'S A FACT!
The trip from Glenn's base in Japan to Ohio took three days. By the time he arrived, Annie was too sick to recognize him.

Annie recovered from her fever, and Glenn returned to Okinawa. He later moved to a base on the Pacific island of Guam, where his family joined him. By this time, Annie had learned to accept the frequent moves and supported her husband's decisions and goals.

GLENN IN KOREA

After the war, Glenn's rank rose from lieutenant to captain to major. He continued to fly at bases in Maryland, California, and the Pacific. At one time, he was assigned to Fighter Squadron 218 in northern China. He flew air patrols when a civil war started in the country. Glenn was about to get involved in another type of war.

The civil war in China was part of the worldwide "Cold War." This war had developed between Communist and non-Communist nations after World War II. The struggle was called the Cold War because it involved little actual fighting. The United States and the Soviet Union and their allies formed two groups. The United States wanted a world of independent, democratic nations. The Soviet Union wanted the government to have control of much of the economy. In

China, the Communists won the civil war. The Cold War was also one reason for fighting in nearby Korea, which had been divided into North Korea and South Korea after World War II. In North Korea, a Communist group fought to overthrow the democratic government of South Korea.

In 1950, the United States entered the Korean conflict. Communist forces in the North had invaded much of South Korea. They were threatening to overrun the country. The United Nations (UN), which had formed in 1945 to work for international peace and security, didn't want the invaders to succeed. The UN sent troops to fight the invaders. Because the United States strongly opposed Communism, Americans made up most of this force.

The Korean War continued for several years. During this time, Glenn served as a flight instructor at Corpus Christi. He also took a class in amphibious warfare, learning how to fight on water and land, at the Marine base in Quantico, Virginia. In February 1953, Glenn went to Korea to join Marine Corps Fighter Squadron 311. The squadron flew F9F Panther jets. These jet fighters

carried machine guns and
heavy bombs. Glenn flew
many missions over
Korea. He later asked to
be moved to a U.S. Air
Force squadron that was
flying F-86 Sabre jet
fighter planes. On July 12,
1953, Glenn had his first
victory in an aerial
dogfight (a fight between
fighter planes at close
range). Glenn shot down
a Soviet-made MiG
fighter. He shot down two

IT'S A FACT!

U.S. military planes
often carry names as
well as initials.
Planes whose names
start with "F" are
fighter planes. An
F-86 Sabre is such a
plane. They engage
the enemy in the air.
Bombers start with
"B," as in a B-25. The
mission of these
planes is to bomb
targets.

more MiGs within the next two weeks, when the war ended.

During World War II and the Korean War, Glenn had flown 149 missions. He had survived antiaircraft fire and one-on-one air combat without injury. He was awarded five Distinguished Flying Crosses for his skill. The awards proved that he was a brave and skilled pilot.

3 PUSHING THE ENVELOPE

(Above) Major John Glenn with a plane he flew in the Korean War. It has many bullet holes in it.

DURING THE KOREAN WAR, Glenn had flown the fastest, newest fighter planes the United States had. After the war, he thought the best way to continue flying was to become a test pilot. These brave fliers are the first to pilot newly designed airplanes. Sometimes the new planes have problems, so testing them is risky. Glenn asked to be moved to the Patuxent River Naval Air Station in Maryland. This station, nicknamed "Pax River," trained former combat pilots to become test pilots.

Glenn had performed well in Korea. But

he still had to convince the officers at Pax River
that he was right for their program. Two of his
former commanders recommended him. Glenn was
accepted, but he needed advanced math skills. He
had not studied math during his two years in college,
so he had to work hard to learn the math he needed.
His work and determination paid off. He graduated
from Pax River as a test pilot in August 1954.

Test pilots at Pax River and at Edwards Air Force
Base in California were flying higher and faster than
ever. On October 14, 1947, Captain Chuck Yaeger
became the first pilot to fly
faster than the speed of
sound. Yaeger had flown in
a rocket plane called the
X1. The U.S. Air Force
started to build jet planes
that could fly faster than
sound. The new models
included the F100 Super
Sabre and the B58 Hustler.

At Pax River, Glenn
flew the new F8U Crusader.
His job was to "push the
envelope," or to take risks.

IT'S A FACT!

The term "push the
envelope" came from
the airplane industry.
The limits of a
plane's way of flying
were marked on a
graph. The "envelope"
was the area of the
graph that showed
safe flying altitudes
and speeds. Flying
outside this area was
risky or unsafe.

He had to fly his planes as high and as fast as they could go. He showed how well they handled at high speeds. He learned the speeds where they would stall or begin to fall. It was hard, dangerous work. Dozens of test pilots died in crashes. Others quit because of the pressure. But Glenn loved the challenge and excitement.

OPERATION BULLET

Glenn flew for two years with no accidents or damage to his planes. In 1956, he was moved to a desk job at the Bureau of Aeronautics in Washington, D.C. He was part of the Fighter Design Branch. It was a safer job, but Glenn missed flying. He still wanted to continue a career as a military pilot.

Through people he knew in Washington, Glenn learned about a project that would take a jet plane called a Crusader from coast to coast at top speeds. He used his personal and political skills to get the assignment as the project's pilot. He nicknamed the project Operation Bullet and created a flight plan for the plane. The plan laid out the schedule for the takeoff, landing, and midair refueling.

On July 16, 1957, Glenn took off from Los

John Glenn was the first person to fly across the United States at speeds faster than the speed of sound.

Alamitos Naval Air Station in California. He flew the Crusader to a height of fifty thousand feet, equal to almost ten miles. He followed a course that took him east and north. He flew over his hometown of New Concord. The Crusader reached speeds of more than one thousand miles per hour. Glenn was flying one and a half times the speed of sound. Three times, the Crusader slowed and dropped to twenty-five thousand feet to refuel in midair. Glenn landed at

Glenn's wife Annie and their children, David and Lyn, greet him after his record-breaking flight in July 1957.

Bennett Field in Brooklyn, New York, three hours, 23 minutes, and 8.4 seconds after takeoff. He had set a new transcontinental speed record. Annie, Dave, and Lyn were there to greet him.

Overnight, Operation Bullet turned Glenn from an unknown test pilot into a hero. He went on a speaking tour and saw himself in newspapers and magazines. People liked his patriotism and enthusiasm. They felt his flight was heroic and an important military achievement.

Even though Glenn had succeeded in World War II and Korea as a combat pilot, his test-

piloting successes meant more. Such achievements
had begun to replace air and land victories as a
measure of success during the Cold War. The
United States and the Soviet Union were still
competing. Each was building bigger, more
powerful planes, tanks, ships, and weapons. The
most powerful of these weapons could destroy the
whole planet. People thought Glenn's flight showed
how daring and able the U.S. military was. Maybe
it would give the United States an edge.

Secretary of the Navy Thomas Gates pins the Distinguished Flying Cross on Glenn in 1957.

THE SPACE RACE

The United States and the Soviet Union were more or less equal with air, land, and sea weapons. The next phase of their Cold War competition was the race for space. Both sides wanted to be the first to send aircraft into space. To prepare for this, the U.S. military built new, powerful rockets. These rockets included the Jupiter, the Viking, and the Redstone. They would one day be able to carry weapons into space.

The U.S. Air Force designed the X-15B spacecraft. Its mission was to carry two pilots into orbit around Earth. Planning moved slowly. By the

fall of 1957, the flights were still just plans. Then on October 4, the

The Soviet satellite *Sputnik* was about 22 inches around and weighed about 184 pounds.

Soviet Union launched *Sputnik,* the first artificial satellite, into space. *Sputnik* was about the size of a beach ball and could carry out only simple radio communication from space. Still, the launch put the Soviets ahead of the United States in the space race.

Two months later, the Soviets launched *Sputnik II.* This larger craft carried a small dog named Laika as a passenger. The satellite circled Earth several times before returning. The flight proved that an animal could survive in space. Laika, however, died during the return.

Many Americans saw *Sputnik* as more than just a scientific achievement. They also saw it as a threat. They thought the Soviet Union might have the ability to attack from space. In response, U.S. military and government leaders wanted to quickly launch a U.S. rocket. On December 6, 1957, a Vanguard rocket carrying a small satellite prepared to launch from Cape Canaveral, on the coast of Florida. The countdown began. At zero, the rocket lifted a few inches from its launching pad. It then stalled, fell back to the ground, and exploded. The launch failure threw the United States into a panic.

In 1958, the U.S. government created the National Aeronautics and Space Administration

(NASA) to plan space missions. NASA would build launch vehicles and satellites and train crew members, called astronauts. Test pilots like Glenn were likely to become the first astronauts.

Scientists and engineers were also part of the NASA team. NASA officials didn't want to continue the X-15B program. Instead, they planned a spacecraft—shaped like a capsule—that could be launched into the sky like a bullet. NASA decided to use the Redstone and Atlas rocket boosters to launch the craft, which would orbit Earth and then return to the ground.

MERCURY MAN

NASA's goal was to put a man in space by the middle of 1960. The program was named Mercury, after the Roman god of travel. NASA would select test pilots to become the astronauts. The candidates could be no older than thirty-nine. They could be no taller than five feet eleven inches. They had to have 1,500 hours of flight time. They also needed a college degree. This requirement disqualified Chuck Yaeger, the nation's most skilled test pilot. He had been the first to break the sound barrier.

GETTING INTO SPACE

To go into orbit and circle the Earth, a spacecraft needs enough speed to escape Earth's gravity. Rockets gave the Mercury capsules the speed they needed to enter orbit. Once the spacecraft is in orbit, it continues to circle Earth. The force of gravity keeps it from floating away.

To return to Earth, the craft must slow down using retro-rockets. These rockets fire in the same direction the spacecraft is flying. Gravity then causes it to fall back toward Earth.

As a spacecraft falls, it enters Earth's atmosphere. This layer of gas surrounds the planet. Once the craft has broken through the upper atmosphere, the astronaut releases parachutes. These help the craft float down to a safe landing.

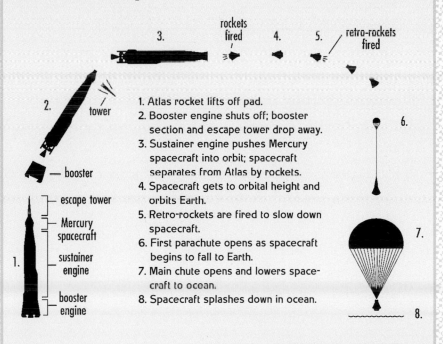

3. rockets fired   4.   5.   retro-rockets fired

2. tower

booster

escape tower

Mercury spacecraft

1.

sustainer engine

booster engine

1. Atlas rocket lifts off pad.
2. Booster engine shuts off; booster section and escape tower drop away.
3. Sustainer engine pushes Mercury spacecraft into orbit; spacecraft separates from Atlas by rockets.
4. Spacecraft gets to orbital height and orbits Earth.
5. Retro-rockets are fired to slow down spacecraft.
6. First parachute opens as spacecraft begins to fall to Earth.
7. Main chute opens and lowers spacecraft to ocean.
8. Spacecraft splashes down in ocean.

6.

7.

8.

The test pilots soon learned that their piloting skills were not that important, because the craft was controlled from the ground. As writer Tom Wolfe described it, a Project Mercury astronaut "would be a human cannonball. He would not be able to alter the course of the capsule in the slightest. The capsule would go up like a cannonball and come down like a cannonball, splashing into the ocean, with a parachute to slow it down and spare the life of the human specimen inside."

IT'S A FACT!

Tom Wolfe wrote his novel *The Right Stuff* in the late 1970s. The public and private lifestyles of test pilots and of the Mercury astronauts were the subject. In the book, John Glenn came across as squeaky clean.

Despite the fact that the pilots wouldn't exactly be flying the spacecrafts, many pilots signed up for the program. They saw it as a way to advance their careers. This is how Glenn saw it—as a great opportunity—when he heard about the program. He was still working at the Bureau of Aeronautics in Washington, D.C, but he eagerly signed up.

Glenn knew he would have problems getting into the Mercury program. He was thirty-eight years old, older than most of the other pilots. He was also six feet tall with a stocky build. He might be too heavy for a Mercury capsule. Like Yaeger, he didn't have a college degree.

Glenn tried to join the program anyway. He also asked his old commanding officers for recommendations. Colonel Jake Dill from Pax River was one of these officers. Dill wanted at least one Marine pilot to make the program. He went to NASA headquarters to insist that Glenn be accepted.

Glenn's lack of a college degree was a problem. He had spent only two years at Muskingum College. But he had also spent a year studying math at Pax River. NASA officials liked

IT'S A FACT!

Glenn badly wanted to get into the Mercury program. But he didn't fit the basic needs. He put himself through hard workouts to lose weight. He spent hours walking around with a stack of books on his head. He wanted to shrink himself below the height limit.

how hard Glenn had worked to master complicated math. So, despite the lack of a degree, he was among the 110 men chosen to enter the program. The next challenge was to make it through the interviews. The final group, or finalists, would go through a lot of tests. The astronauts would be the best of the finalists.

CHAPTER 4

GETTING WITH THE PROGRAM

As soon as NASA officials had the team together, they interviewed each candidate. They explained the Mercury program. Each pilot answered questions about his life and career. The pilots talked about how they felt about taking risks. The pilots also had to think about how the program would affect their careers. Many of them still thought that piloted rocket planes like the X-15B would one day be common. The Mercury vehicles looked and flew nothing like the X-15B. Advanced piloting skills would not be of much use in the capsules.

The program was also dangerous. Astronauts were putting their lives and careers at risk. But the mission was important to the U.S. government and military. The top goal was to put a man in space before the Soviets. Mercury was the fastest way to do so. If the astronauts returned home safely, they would be heroes.

TESTING AND MORE TESTING

NASA split the finalists into groups and then moved them to the Lovelace Clinic in Albuquerque, New Mexico. Doctors at the clinic tested the pilots' blood, strength, and reflexes. They took X-rays. The doctors did not explain the purpose of these tests. In fact, NASA's doctors were not too worried about fitness. They knew all the finalists were strong and healthy. Instead, NASA wanted to learn how much pain the pilots could stand. They wanted to see how well they might perform in space. The Lovelace Clinic was the last stop in the program for some candidates. Many didn't like being space guinea pigs and quit in frustration, pain, and anger.

IT'S A FACT!

One of the candidates, Donald "Deke" Slayton, wrote: "While I thought the Lovelace physical examinations were excessive, I could at least see the point. But the idea behind all these so-called 'stress' tests at Wright-Patterson escaped me completely...."

NASA next measured each man's ability to withstand the stress of spaceflight. Glenn and the others went to Wright-Patterson Air Force Base, near Dayton, Ohio, for more tests. The candidates sat in spaceflight simulators. These machines created the heavy vibrations, bumpiness, and high g-forces expected during the Mercury flights. (One g is equal to the force of gravity on the body at rest. Higher g-forces occur during rapid speed changes, which put great pressure on the body.) The candidates withstood extreme heat and cold. They were jarred by loud noises. They spent long periods lying flat on their backs. It was the position they would be in while inside the capsule. NASA even put the men into a room with no light or sound for several hours.

MEDIA AND THE MERCURY SEVEN

The testing went on for months. Finally, on April 9, 1959, NASA held a press conference to announce the seven astronauts. At a long table sat the "Mercury Seven"–Wally Schirra, Scott Carpenter, Alan Shepard, Gus Grissom, Deke Slayton, Gordon Cooper, and John Glenn. Photographers snapped pictures while reporters asked the astronauts questions about the

NASA introduces the first U.S. astronauts. *From left to right:* **Scott Carpenter, Gordon Cooper, John Glenn, Virgil (Gus) Grissom, Walter Schirra, Alan Shepard, and Donald (Deke) Slayton.**

risks of spaceflight. They asked the astronauts if they worried about leaving their families for such a dangerous mission. Several of the men grew uncomfortable with such personal questions.

Glenn didn't mind the questions and showed he was good at dealing with the media. Later, Deke Slayton wrote that "the real surprise was watching John Glenn. He ate this stuff up. Somebody asked if our wives were behind us. Six of us said, 'Sure,' as if that had ever been a real consideration. Glenn piped up with a . . . speech about God and family and destiny. We all looked at him, and then at each other." Glenn's confidence soon made him an unofficial leader of the group. Reporters knew they could always go to him for a good quote.

NASA knew that the public attention could become a problem. Reporters always wanted to talk to the astronauts and might go to strange lengths to get a story. NASA decided to sell the rights for the astronauts' stories to one bidder.

Glenn, *third from left*, showed a natural talent for dealing with reporters.

A New York lawyer named Leo DeOrsey served as the astronauts' agent. He sold the rights to *Life* magazine for $500,000. The astronauts agreed to split the money. In exchange, *Life* was allowed to interview the astronauts and write about their lives. Glenn and the others could talk to anyone about the mission, but they could only talk to *Life* about their personal lives. The magazine ran a series of stories about the astronauts that gave the public the image of hardworking, clean-cut heroes. The deal made some of *Life*'s competitors unhappy, but the astronauts benefited from the arrangement.

TRAINING AND PROBLEMS

The Mercury Seven moved near Langley Air Force Base in Virginia, where NASA had set up its headquarters. From this base, the group traveled around the country. They learned about the different parts of the Mercury program. In Saint Louis, Missouri, they saw the Mercury capsules being built. They toured the launch area at Cape Canaveral. In Huntsville, Alabama, they saw the Redstone rockets. They looked at the Atlas rockets at a plant in San Diego, California.

A Redstone rocket blasts off.

The astronauts had to learn many new details and skills. But because no single man could learn everything, each man learned about an area of the Mercury flights. Deke Slayton was in charge of the Atlas rocket. Gordon Copper learned about the Redstone. Wally Schirra was assigned pressure suits. Al Shepard studied ways to track the capsule from the ground and recover it at sea. Scott Carpenter handled navigation and radio communications. Gus Grissom studied the thrusters. John Glenn's area was the inside design of the spacecraft. He studied

Glenn at Langley Field, Virginia. Some of the Mercury capsule's controls can be seen through the windows.

the controls, switches, and gauges that would be used in flight.

NASA wanted to launch as soon as possible. The agency planned to make a series of flights on a Redstone rocket in early 1960. These flights would take the spacecraft far up into the atmosphere. But it would not go high enough to enter orbit. Later, NASA would switch to short orbital flights.

NASA wanted the program to finish in 1961, but problems delayed it. The Atlas rocket failed on four out of every ten test launches. Tests of an empty Mercury capsule also failed. On July 19, 1960, a countdown began at Cape Canaveral for the launch of Mercury-Atlas 1. It was the beginning of the program's official flights. An Atlas rocket was supposed to carry a complete Mercury capsule. NASA hoped the launch would show the conditions of spaceflight. One minute after the launch, thirty-two thousand feet in the air, the Atlas exploded.

NASA worked to solve the problems with the Atlas. Glenn and the other astronauts continued their training. They worked in simulators and pressure chambers to know what spaceflight would

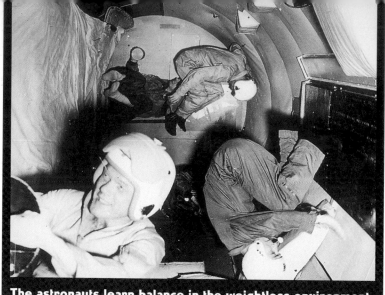

The astronauts learn balance in the weightless environment of a transport plane. Glenn is at front left.

feel like. They learned about underwater diving for splashdowns on the return flight. They studied desert survival because the missions took them over the Sahara Desert in Africa. They also flew on C-47 planes at Holloman Air Force Base in New Mexico. When pilots flew the planes in high arcs, the astronauts became weightless for a short time and got some experience of being free of Earth's gravity.

IT'S A FACT!

To make the 1995 movie *Apollo 13*, director Ron Howard needed a way to re-create weightlessness. NASA allowed him to film aboard its astronaut training aircraft. It used the same principle as the C-47 to create the actual experience of weightlessness for the actors.

A DISAPPOINTING CHOICE

In the fall of 1960, John F. Kennedy was elected president. By this time, the public knew NASA more for its failures and delays than for its space exploration. The Soviet space program was far more successful. NASA officials worried that Kennedy might cancel the Mercury program. They pushed ahead quickly with more tests. Officials also wanted to name an astronaut for the first flight. It would be a short flight high in the atmosphere using a Redstone rocket.

Bob Gilruth was the director of the group that was training the Mercury astronauts. He held a peer vote among the Mercury Seven. Each astronaut had to vote for the best man to take the first flight. As Tom Wolfe explains, "Peer votes were not unknown in the military . . . but peer votes had never amounted to anything more than . . . an indication of how men at the same level regarded one another, whether for reasons of professionalism or friendship or jealousy or whatever. Pilots regarded peer votes as a waste of time, because a man either had the right stuff in the air or he didn't, and a military career . . . was not a personality contest."

Glenn thought he was a good choice to take the first flight. He had done well in training and in simulations. He knew all about the flight plan and controls. But he also knew he might have trouble with a vote. Some of the others did not like the way he took a leadership role. They resented his clean-cut image. He worked constantly to outshine them in flight training and physical workouts. Glenn was an excellent pilot, but he was also an ambitious political climber who knew how to use his people skills to impress his superiors.

Glenn was right to worry about a vote. The astronauts voted for Alan Shepard to take the flight. On January 19, 1961, NASA announced the lineup for the first Mercury flight. Shepard would ride the capsule, with Gus Grissom and John Glenn as backups.

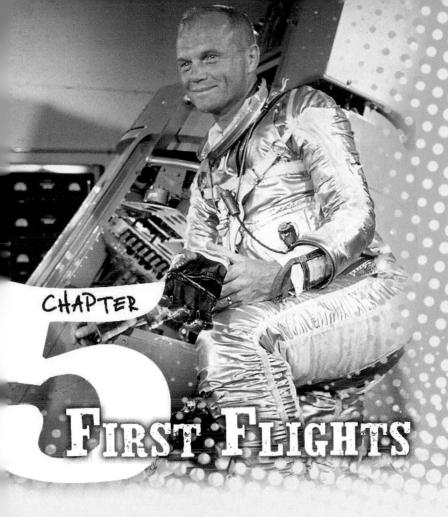

CHAPTER

5 FIRST FLIGHTS

GLENN WAS DISAPPOINTED and angry that the other astronauts picked Shepard. He felt that he had been cheated of his mission because he was unpopular.

At Cape Canaveral, he continued to prepare. He wanted to be ready in case

(Above)
John Glenn standing beside a Mercury capsule during training

49

anything happened to Shepard and Grissom. The selection had not been announced to the public yet. Because he was more comfortable with the media, Glenn got more attention. As a result, many people in the media believed that NASA would select Glenn. He had to keep smiling in public, but at home, he was angry and kept to himself. His family didn't even know why.

Meanwhile, the United States was falling farther behind in the space race. On April 12, 1961, a Soviet cosmonaut (astronaut) named Yuri Gagarin lifted off in the capsule *Vostok 1*. Gagarin became the first person to orbit Earth and return safely.

Shepard's flight, called Mercury 3, was scheduled for May 2, 1961. Bad weather stopped the liftoff. NASA tried again on May 5. At 9:49 A.M., *Freedom 7* was launched. After the Redstone booster separated, the capsule made a high arc. It reached 116.5 miles in the air. Fifteen minutes after the launch, Shepard splashed down in the Atlantic Ocean, three hundred miles from the launchpad. The United States had completed its first crewed space mission. On July 21, Gus Grissom made the second crewed Mercury flight in a capsule he called the *Liberty Bell 7*. Even

Gus Grissom prepares to enter the *Liberty Bell 7* spacecraft in July 1961 before rocketing 118 miles into space.

though the United States had sent two men into space, neither mission equaled the Soviet Union's progress.

FRIENDSHIP 7

NASA and Glenn prepared for another short mission. But on August 6, the Soviet Union took another important step ahead of the United States. Cosmonaut Gherman Titov orbited Earth sixteen times in *Vostok 2*, spending more than a day in space.

Pressure from the public and the U.S. Congress grew. NASA planners decided they needed to send Glenn into orbit using the Atlas rocket. NASA tested the Atlas rocket in the fall of 1961. One test flight on November 28, 1961, carried a chimpanzee named Enos. The flight was a success.

Glenn's flight, named Mercury-Atlas 6, was scheduled for December 1961. But problems fitting the Mercury capsule atop the much larger Atlas booster delayed the launch. On January 16,

1962, problems with the fuel tanks caused another delay. Bad weather stopped the mission on January 23. Four days later, Glenn spent five hours suited up and ready inside the capsule, but heavy clouds stopped the launch.

On February 20, 1962, Glenn again prepared for launch. This time, the weather was clear. At 9:47 A.M., the ninety-five-foot Atlas rocket started, and *Friendship 7* took off from Cape

Friendship 7 takes off from Cape Canaveral, Florida, in February 1962 to orbit Earth.

Canaveral. The Atlas lifted and turned toward the east. The capsule shook as it sped up. The force of 6 g's made Glenn's body feel like it weighed hundreds of pounds more than his real weight. Glenn had experienced high g-forces many times before in simulators. After reaching a speed of 17,500 miles an hour, the capsule broke away from the booster rocket. At about 550,000 feet, *Friendship 7* was in orbit.

The g-forces decreased until Glenn was weightless. "Zero g and I feel fine," he told ground controllers. Glenn enthusiastically described what he was seeing by talking into his "capcom," or capsule communicator. He said, "The speed at which the sun goes down is remarkable. The white line of the horizon, sandwiched between the black sky and dark Earth, is extremely bright as the sun sets. As the sun goes down a little bit more, the bottom layer becomes orange, and it fades into red and finally off into blues and black as you look farther up into space."

Glenn kept going through his spaceflight routine. He went over checklists and gauge readings while *Friendship 7* crossed over the Pacific Ocean. NASA had planned for *Friendship 7* to make seven full orbits of Earth. Each one would take about one and a half hours.

The capsule was not working correctly, though. One of the thrusters that controlled the capsule was broken. Glenn felt the capsule swing back and forth as the other thrusters fired. He switched to manual control, but he knew that if he didn't fix the problem, he'd have to point the capsule for reentry himself. He would also have to save fuel until the end of the flight. The capsule would fly out of control if it didn't have enough fuel.

Flight engineers on the ground noticed another problem. A sensor reported that the

Flight engineers watch as *Friendship 7* passes over Australia.

landing bag on the end of the capsule had
deployed, or opened up. But the ground
controllers couldn't be sure. The sensor might
have been broken. The bag was placed
underneath the heat shield and wasn't supposed to
be used until reentry. If it had deployed, the heat
shield on *Friendship 7* might come loose. Without
the shield, the capsule would burn up before
splashdown.

The ground controllers didn't tell Glenn
about the landing bag until his third orbit. They
asked him twice if the landing bag switch was off.
Both times, Glenn reported that it was. Finally,
they had Glenn put the switch in the "automatic"
position. A light inside *Friendship 7* would show
whether the bag had really deployed.

Glenn was surprised and angry that they had
not told him right away. He knew that if the
landing bag was in its proper position, throwing
the switch might deploy it accidentally. He
moved his gloved hand slowly toward the
control. He flipped the switch and watched the
indicator. "Negative," he reported. "In automatic
position, did not get a light, and I'm back in off
position now. Over."

This photo of Glenn was taken with an automatic camera inside the *Friendship 7* capsule as he was orbiting Earth.

The flight was almost done. Glenn had to use the retro-rockets on the back of *Friendship 7* to aim the spacecraft. If he aimed it wrong, the flight would end in disaster. NASA asked Glenn to fire the retro-rockets but to keep them in place, instead of letting them float away into space. The strap holding the rockets might also help to hold the heat shield in place. Without the heat shield, the spacecraft would burn up in the atmosphere.

Glenn obeyed the orders. He checked the capsule's angle and then fired the retro-rockets to slow the spacecraft. A cloud of flames and gas surrounded *Friendship 7* as it entered the atmosphere. The heat caused radio communication to go out.

Outside his window, Glenn saw chunks of hot metal flying away from the capsule. He didn't know right away what the pieces were. The inside of the capsule started to become hot, but Glenn didn't worry. He had figured out that the pieces of metal were the retro-rockets, which he no longer needed.

IT'S A FACT!

On his reentry into Earth's atmosphere, Glenn said, "Boy, that was a real fireball of a ride."

Two parachutes opened above the capsule. A green light showed Glenn that the landing bag had deployed just as it was supposed to.

At 2:43 P.M., *Friendship 7* splashed down in the Atlantic Ocean eight hundred miles southeast of Cape Canaveral. The flight was over. Glenn had made three orbits in four hours and fifty-six minutes of spaceflight.

A fleet of ships circled the landing zone, near Grand Turk Island in the Caribbean Sea. The ships searched for *Friendship 7*. Glenn remained inside the capsule, bobbing in the waves. Heat built up inside the capsule and inside his suit. After twenty-one minutes, a helicopter picked up the capsule. The helicopter set it safely on the deck of the destroyer *Noa*.

CHAPTER 6
A FLIGHT INTO POLITICS

THE FLIGHT OF *Friendship* 7 had been a success. Glenn had made three orbits and had returned home safely. But NASA had hoped for better. Too many problems had come up on the mission. The United States had a long way to go before it could catch up with the Soviet space program.

(Above) Sailors guide *Friendship 7* aboard the recovery ship, *Noa,* after Glenn's successful flight.

At home, people again saw Glenn as a hero. Finally, the U.S. space program seemed to be moving forward. Glenn's flight was a success after many disappointments. People liked Glenn, and they saw him as a hardworking, clean-cut, all-American man. "The attention lavished on him by the nation . . . could not be explained solely by the glamour of his flight," wrote journalist Frank Van Riper. "There seemed to be a quality about Glenn that attracted the public; an appearance, background and attitude which conjured up a view of the country that was equal parts fantasy and nostalgia."

President Kennedy had also noticed these qualities in Glenn. Kennedy had served in World War II as a naval officer. He admired men who had courage and a sense of duty. He saw Glenn as more than just an astronaut. Kennedy thought Glenn might be a valuable political friend in the upcoming presidential election of 1964.

Next Steps

Kennedy flew to Cape Canaveral after the flight of *Friendship 7*. He congratulated Glenn in a ceremony there. He then flew Glenn and his family back to

President John Kennedy *(at podium)* presented Glenn *(at Kennedy's left)* with the NASA Distinguished Service Award in 1962. Next to Glenn are his wife Annie, his daughter Lyn, and his son David.

Washington, D.C., aboard *Air Force One,* the official presidential jet. The president held a reception for Glenn at the White House. At the Capitol Building, Glenn gave a nationally televised speech to Congress. On March 1, 1962, he and the other Mercury astronauts went to New York City. As a sign of welcome, ribbons of paper, called ticker tapes, rained down on the astronauts as they rode through the city.

Glenn's success and fame were good for the Mercury program. Engineers planned more Mercury flights. They also began to work on Kennedy's challenge to send a crewed mission to the moon. The Gemini program would be the next step. Two-person capsules would remain in orbit for several days instead of hours. Astronauts would carry out docking and spacewalking missions.

Glenn hoped he would be selected to take part in the Gemini program. He was over forty, but he thought his experience would help him earn a spot. Kennedy told NASA that he wanted to keep Glenn on the ground. Glenn didn't know it yet, but he had flown his last space mission for many years.

After the flight of *Friendship 7*, Glenn and his family moved to Houston, Texas, where NASA had set up the new Manned Spaceflight Center. Glenn worked as a ground controller. He helped with the Mercury flights of Scott Carpenter, Wally Schirra, and Gordon Cooper. But Glenn already had a new career in mind.

FIRST TRY FOR THE SENATE

Since high school, Glenn had been a good public speaker. During his military service, he had often thought about running for public office. He was ambitious and had a strong sense of duty to his country. He also was a hero and knew that people liked him. He had the friendship and support of President Kennedy. Glenn decided to run for the U.S. Senate to represent Ohio in Congress.

Senator Steve Young, who held one of Ohio's Senate seats, would be running for reelection. Kennedy would also be running for reelection. Kennedy believed that if his friend could win Young's seat, it would help his presidential race. Kennedy promised Young a high government post in exchange for pulling out of the race.

At the time of Glenn's *Friendship 7* flight, President Kennedy was already thinking about the 1964 election.

Young thought about the offer. He was a Democrat like Kennedy and Glenn. But he was seventy-four years old and already thinking about retirement. Still, he enjoyed the Senate and had the support of the Ohio Democratic Party. Young also felt he was already in a good position to win his Senate seat. During the primary election, the Ohio Democrats and Republicans would select their final candidates for the election in the fall. Young believed he already had enough support to win the race.

On November 22, 1963, President Kennedy was killed in Dallas, Texas. Vice President Lyndon Johnson became the new president. Kennedy's deal with Steve Young was off. Robert Kennedy, one of President Kennedy's brothers, told Glenn that it might be best not to run in the election.

Lyndon Johnson (center with hand raised) took the oath as president soon after President Kennedy died.

Glenn had no organization backing him and almost no money. He decided to run for the Senate anyway. But he announced that he was going to run on January 17, three days before the Ohio Democratic convention. It had been almost two years since his Mercury flight. But Glenn believed those five hours in space would be enough to bring him a surprise victory.

Glenn's campaign started slowly. A law called the Hatch Act prevents employees of the U.S. government and members of the military from political activity. Glenn had officially retired from the space program in January, but he was still a Marine. He was not allowed to make political speeches or appear in ads. Instead, Glenn attended the convention, but he remained in his hotel room. He met with delegates who came to his room to meet him and get his autograph.

Glenn impressed many of the delegates, many of whom began to move to his side. A group of Young's supporters feared Glenn's rising popularity. They offered him a place in the House of Representatives if he gave up his challenge to Young. Glenn refused their offer. He wanted a seat in the Senate. Many of the delegates worried that the elderly Young might lose to a Republican candidate in November. They thought Glenn might be a better choice. After taking a vote, the convention was deadlocked. Neither man had won.

Glenn believed he could still win the Senate seat. He decided to quit the Marine Corps. While he waited for the orders to come through, he traveled around Ohio. Crowds of people came to meet him. But they wanted to hear his political ideas. In fact, on many issues, he still hadn't formed an opinion. He had had little time as an astronaut to think about the issues of civil rights, crime, poverty, and education. Instead, Glenn asked the public to give him *their* opinions. Many voters thought Glenn's style was a nice change.

By late February, the campaign was in full swing. Then an accident stopped Glenn's campaign. On February 26, he fell in the bathroom at his apartment in Columbus, Ohio. His head hit the side of the bathtub. The fall caused a concussion and a buildup of fluid in his inner ear. He felt ill and dizzy. He had trouble walking. He spent several weeks in the hospital. During this time, Annie Glenn and Rene Carpenter, the wife of Scott Carpenter,

From his hospital bed, Glenn told the media he was withdrawing from the Senate campaign. He had been put in a hospital after a serious fall in his home.

campaigned in Glenn's place. By March 30, Glenn still wasn't feeling well, so he dropped out of the race. Steve Young went on to beat Republican Robert Taft to hold his seat. Lyndon Johnson won the November presidential election.

What Next?

Glenn returned to his home near Houston to rest and recover. For several months, he could barely walk around the house. Slowly, his health and his balance improved. He was also facing a new problem. He needed a new way to support his family. He still owed sixteen thousand dollars from his campaign. Instead of holding a political fund-raiser to pay the debt, he decided to pay it himself. His decision almost cleared out the family's savings.

John Glenn was still a famous name. Companies offered him money to endorse products or to join their boards of directors. In October 1964, Glenn accepted an offer from the Royal Crown Cola company. He would work as a vice president and serve on the board of directors. Within a short time, he was named president of Royal Crown International. This department sold Royal Crown Cola outside the United States. Glenn moved into an apartment paid for by his employer in New York City.

Glenn also used contacts he had made in Florida to enter the hotel business. He went into partnership with an old friend named Henri Landwirth, who owned land in Cocoa Beach. The two men formed a company to build hotels in Florida. The state was booming with people seeking warm weather. Glenn and Landwirth put in a bid for a Holiday Inn franchise. They wanted the right to build a hotel using the Holiday Inn name. One of these valuable franchises was in Orlando, near the site of the new Disney World theme park.

Glenn and Landwirth were awarded the Orlando franchise and several others. The hotel was a huge success and earned Glenn several hundred thousand dollars a year. Glenn had also accepted positions with several other companies. For these jobs, he only had to take part in board meetings and help decide company policies. In only a few years, Glenn had become very wealthy. But he never forgot his goal to serve in the U.S. Senate.

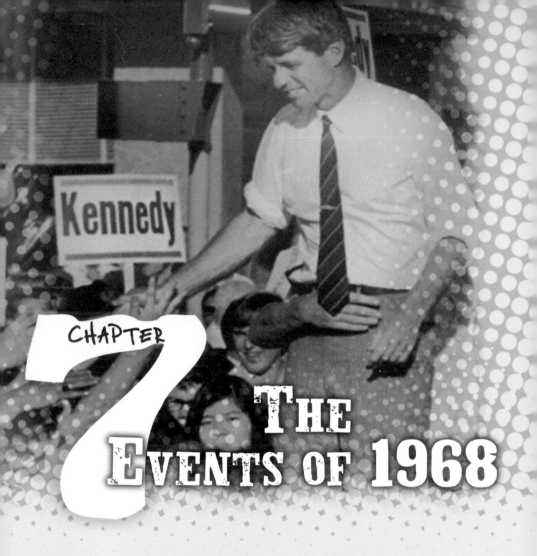

CHAPTER 7

THE EVENTS OF 1968

(Above) Senator Robert Kennedy campaigns for the 1968 Democratic presidential nomination.

GLENN WAS STILL not satisfied with the direction of his life. He wanted to find new challenges. In 1968, he wanted another chance to enter politics. He took an opportunity to join Robert Kennedy's presidential campaign.

Robert Kennedy and Glenn had remained close friends after President

Kennedy's death. Robert Kennedy admired
Glenn's courage and character, while Glenn learned
a lot from Kennedy's grasp of political and social
issues. Kennedy supported civil and voting rights
for minorities. He spoke out for the country's poor.
He also stood against the Vietnam War
(1954–1975), which the United States had entered in
the 1960s. By 1968, the war was dividing the
country. From Robert Kennedy, Glenn learned how
to organize a campaign, raise money, and use the

U.S. soldiers carry their gear through a river in Vietnam.

media. Glenn also hoped that if Kennedy won, he might reward Glenn with a government job.

The final Democratic candidate would be chosen at the Democratic National

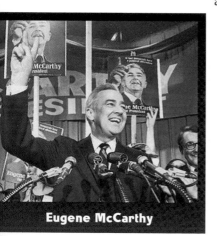

Eugene McCarthy

Convention in the summer of 1968. The winner would run for president against the Republican candidate in the November 1968 election. Public opinion polls showed that President Lyndon Johnson and Senator Eugene McCarthy of Minnesota were in a close race. Many people questioned President Johnson's ability to lead the nation through the Vietnam War and the problems with civil rights.

Before the main election took place in November, the candidates participated in primaries. These are elections that test the popularity of the candidates within the same party. In the March 12 New Hampshire primary, Johnson barely got more votes than McCarthy. This meant Johnson wasn't a clear-cut

Lyndon Johnson

John Glenn *(right)* attends a fund-raiser with Senator Robert Kennedy and his wife Ethel.

first choice for the Democratic nomination. Soon afterward, Robert Kennedy announced that he would also run for the Democratic nomination. On March 31, Lyndon Johnson made a surprising announcement. He had decided to pull out of the race. Johnson's vice president, Hubert Humphrey of Minnesota, then entered the race.

Glenn accepted Robert Kennedy's invitation to join his campaign. Kennedy feared that some people might see him as too liberal. He hoped Glenn's military record and fame would help his image. Glenn supported Kennedy on many issues. But they disagreed about how the United States should approach the Vietnam War. Kennedy wanted to take U.S. troops out of Vietnam. Glenn believed that the government should officially declare war and give the military a better chance to win it.

The race was very close by the time of the California primary on June 5, 1968. California's large population made it an important state. Only New York was bigger. Kennedy earned a very close victory in California. It was just enough to keep him ahead of McCarthy until the Democratic Convention.

Kennedy left his hotel room that night after his victory was announced. He went to the ballroom of the Ambassador Hotel in Los Angeles to give a speech. Glenn remained upstairs.

After finishing the speech, Kennedy left the room. He walked back to the hotel kitchen to avoid the crowd. Suddenly, a short, thin, young man named Sirhan Sirhan appeared. He aimed a pistol at Kennedy's head and fired. The senator fell to the floor, bleeding from a deep bullet wound.

Within seconds of hearing the news, Glenn rushed down to the kitchen. He watched as Kennedy was lifted from the floor and put into an ambulance. He was rushed to a hospital for emergency surgery. Ethel stayed with her husband, who died the next night. John Glenn had lost a close friend and an important political ally. His political career had again come to a stop.

IT'S A FACT!

Ethel Kennedy asked Glenn to break the news of Robert Kennedy's being shot to the six Kennedy children who were in California. Later, Glenn had to tell them that their father had died.

8 BATTLES IN OHIO

THE 1968 PRESIDENTIAL campaign went on, and former vice president Richard Nixon eventually won. Nixon inherited the problems linked to the Vietnam War and the civil rights movement.

(Above) President Nixon greets U.S. troops in South Vietnam.

In 1970, Steve Young announced that he would retire from the U.S. Senate. Glenn saw his chance to get back into politics. To the public, he was still the hero of *Friendship 7*. He was also a successful businessman who had

76

been a friend of Robert Kennedy, one of the most popular Democrats of the 1960s.

A NEAR MISS

Glenn announced that he was going to run for Young's seat. So did Howard Metzenbaum, a Cleveland businessman, former Democratic state lawmaker, and Steve Young's campaign manager. Metzenbaum was not as well known as Glenn. He was also Jewish, and Ohio voters had never elected a Jewish candidate to a major office. But Metzenbaum was an experienced politician. Ohio's strong labor unions supported him. He also had plenty of money and was able to hire professional campaign advisers. He appeared in television ads to make voters familiar with his name and his views.

John Glenn *(left)* and Howard Metzenbaum *(right)* both seek victory in the 1970 Ohio Democratic primary election. The man in the center is not named.

Glenn was still confident. He believed his reputation would be enough to win the Ohio Democratic primary. He had a small staff and didn't spend much money. He wanted to save his money for the race against the Republican nominee. Glenn also decided not to become too close to the Ohio Democratic Party. Many of its members thought Glenn was too conservative.

Glenn soon saw that Metzenbaum was a strong opponent. His experience as a labor lawyer was important to Ohio's strong unions. His views on issues such as welfare, civil rights, and public spending made him popular in large cities. Metzenbaum hired a big staff to spread his message. He was good at raising money. Soon, Metzenbaum's name and face were familiar to Ohio voters.

In his speeches, Metzenbaum criticized President Nixon's handling of the Vietnam War. Glenn's military training had taught him to respect the commander in chief. He would not criticize Nixon, even though he disagreed with him on the way the United States was fighting the war. On May 4, 1970, the day before the Democratic primary, Vietnam became even more important in voters' minds. On that day, students at Kent State

The Ohio National Guard march on Kent State University in 1970 as students protest U.S. involvement in the Vietnam War.

University in Ohio were protesting the war. Members of the Ohio National Guard shot and killed four of the students. The shootings shocked voters. Many of them began to side with Metzenbaum on the issue. On May 5, Glenn won almost all of Ohio's rural counties, but Metzenbaum did well in the big cities and won the primary.

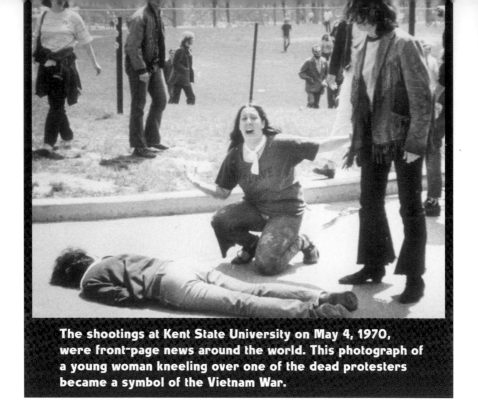

The shootings at Kent State University on May 4, 1970, were front-page news around the world. This photograph of a young woman kneeling over one of the dead protesters became a symbol of the Vietnam War.

Glenn had again missed a chance to serve in the Senate. This time, there had been no accident. He could only blame the way he had run his campaign. Glenn then joined the campaign of John Gilligan, who was running for Ohio governor. He made speeches for Gilligan and appeared in his ads. That

November, Gilligan won the governor's race.
Metzenbaum lost his race to Robert Taft Jr.

LOOKING AHEAD

Many people believed Glenn's political career had
ended. But Glenn was looking forward to the 1974
election. Republican senator William Saxbe would
be running for reelection. Glenn had learned from
his earlier campaigns. He knew that he had to be
more involved in politics to win an election. His
fame was not enough. Glenn moved to Columbus,
the state capital, and made Ohio his permanent
home. He was more active in the state Democratic
organization. Governor Gilligan rewarded Glenn for
his campaign work by appointing him to an

John Glenn *(left)*, chair of
the Ohio Citizen's Task
Force on Environmental
Protection, presents a
copy of his report to
Governor John Gilligan
(right).

environmental task force (a group with a specific task to accomplish). Glenn helped to write a new law setting up a state environmental agency. He also traveled around the state. He made speeches, met the public, did favors, and worked on gaining support for his next campaign.

During the 1972 presidential campaign between Nixon and George McGovern, politics in the United States changed. Someone had broken into the Democratic National Committee headquarters in Washington, D.C. People suspected Nixon's supporters. Nixon's reelection didn't stop the investigators. The investigation led to several high-level job resignations. One resignation was of the country's attorney general, or chief law enforcer.

Senator William Saxbe replaced the attorney general. He had to resign his Ohio Senate seat to take the job. Governor Gilligan had to choose someone to replace the senator. Both John Glenn and Howard Metzenbaum wanted the job. Gilligan did not want to choose Glenn. He hoped Glenn would be his running mate in the 1974 governor's election. Gilligan also thought that choosing Metzenbaum was a good political move. It could

Attorney General William Saxbe *(left)* with President Richard Nixon *(right)*

gain him the support of the labor unions. Again, Glenn was disappointed.

Glenn was not interested in running as Gilligan's lieutenant governor. He announced that he would run for the Senate in 1974 with or without Gilligan's help. Within months, Glenn and Metzenbaum were battling again for the Ohio Democratic nomination for the Senate.

CHAPTER 9

ROOKIE IN THE SENATE

THE RACE BETWEEN John Glenn and Howard Metzenbaum was rough and bitter. This time, Glenn knew he had to work to win. His opponent had the support of the state's Democratic Party and most of the Democratic voters.

Glenn still had no experience as an elected official. He relied on his military record and his experience as an astronaut. He criticized Metzenbaum's much safer career as a lawyer and businessman. (The military had turned down Metzenbaum for active service during World War II because of his poor eyesight.) Metzenbaum pointed to his public service as a state lawmaker. He had been the youngest member of the Ohio House of Representatives in history. He had fought against discrimination and for workers' rights in the 1940s and 1950s, when such views were far less popular.

Glenn toured the state in a bus. He stopped at shopping malls, senior citizens' homes, factories, and anywhere he could find voters. At each stop, he shook hands and made speeches. But early polls showed that Glenn was not gaining on Metzenbaum. In February 1974, Glenn hired Steve Kovacik, an experienced manager, to run his campaign. He told Glenn not to worry so much about small towns, which Kovacik thought Glenn would win anyway. Instead, Kovacik sent Glenn to Ohio's cities, where he would try to take away some of Metzenbaum's supporters among union members and minorities.

Kovacik told Glenn to talk about Metzenbaum's wealth. Glenn also talked about how his opponent found legal ways to avoid paying taxes. Glenn released his own tax records to prove that he had paid more taxes than Metzenbaum, even though he had earned much less. Metzenbaum was embarrassed. People questioned his honesty. Glenn asked him to release his own tax records. He tried to make people question Metzenbaum's morals.

Metzenbaum responded by accusing Glenn of being too conservative. He said Glenn's views didn't always fit with the Democratic Party. He also suggested that Glenn had never held a real job. It was Metzenbaum's way of saying that Glenn had worked for the government most of his life.

Glenn knew he had to respond to Metzenbaum's remark. He made a speech that talked about brave soldiers who had risked their lives fighting for the United States. The speech made headlines across the state. It helped to give Glenn a victory by ninety-one thousand votes. That November, Glenn easily beat his Republican challenger, Ralph Perk of Cleveland. He won every county in Ohio. Finally, John Glenn was a U.S. senator.

John Glenn flashes a big smile after becoming the Democratic nominee for the U.S. Senate in Ohio. He went on to beat Republican Ralph Perk in the Senate race in November 1974.

LEARNING THE ROPES

In January 1975, Glenn joined ninety-nine other senators in Congress. He spent many hours in his Senate office. He studied books and papers on current issues, such as education, taxes, and the military. He also learned about the different Senate committees that help to form laws on specific issues. Much of the Senate's work takes place in these committees.

Like every new senator, Glenn asked senior members of his party for committee assignments that interested him. These senior members eventually appointed him to the Armed Services Committee, the Governmental Affairs Committee, and the Senate Select Intelligence Committee. The longer Glenn served on the committees, the more seniority, or power, he had.

Glenn was one of the most famous members of the Senate. But he did not always get along with the other senators. Most senators were willing to make deals to get what they wanted. Glenn didn't like to make deals to get new laws passed. He also had trouble raising money. He didn't like going to fund-raising events where he met people in order to get donations of money.

Politics in the United States continued to change. On the morning of August 9, 1974, Nixon resigned as president. (Investigations of the earlier break-in of the Democratic Party's headquarters had shown guilt on the part of Nixon and his staff.) At noon that day, Vice President Gerald Ford became president of the United States.

Many politicians wanted the public to see them as "outsiders," who were not a part of "politics as usual" in Washington, D.C. Glenn had a reputation as an outsider. So did Georgia's governor Jimmy Carter, who had no experience in Washington. Carter quickly became the front-runner to be the Democrats' presidential candidate in the 1976 election.

Party leaders asked Glenn to be one of the Democratic National Conventions keynote speakers. He would give a speech in front of the entire convention. It was an important role. Many people believed that Carter might even choose Glenn as his vice presidential running mate.

On July 12, Glenn stood at the podium in New York's Madison Square Garden, the site of the convention. His job was to praise the Democratic Party and its programs on national television. He

Senator John Glenn gives a speech at the 1976 Democratic National Convention.

was supposed to get Democratic voters across the country excited about their candidate. Instead, Glenn talked about making government more responsive to the voters. He didn't praise the Democrats, nor did he attack the Republicans. His speech was dry and flat, and the audience was bored. Many delegates got out of their seats to walk around and do something else. After Glenn finished his speech, few people applauded.

IT'S A FACT!

At the convention, Glenn spoke after Congresswoman Barbara Jordan gave a speech. Her talk was full of emotion and passion. As Glenn said in his autobiography, "I knew I was in trouble. Jordan was a very hard act to follow."

Jimmy Carter had watched the speech. He then went over a list of names he had of possible running mates. He had already decided to choose a member of Congress. He had met with three of his choices at his home in Plains, Georgia. They were John Glenn, Walter Mondale from Minnesota, and Edmund Muskie from Maine. During the meeting, Mondale and Carter had become friends. Carter was already leaning toward Mondale, but Glenn's long, boring speech made his decision easier.

In November 1976, Jimmy Carter won the

Jimmy Carter *(left)* chose Walter Mondale *(right)*, rather than Glenn, as his running mate in the 1976 presidential campaign.

presidential election. Glenn continued his work in
the Senate, where he supported most of Carter's
programs. He gave short speeches in the Senate
chamber, attended meetings, and welcomed visitors
from his home state. Although he was still a rookie,
Glenn enjoyed success as a lawmaker. His
amendments (changes to laws) won ten roll-call
votes during his first year. Roll-call votes are held
when voice votes are too close to call. The voters of
Ohio were satisfied with the job Glenn was doing,
and they reelected him to the Senate in 1980.

NEW CHALLENGES

By the 1980s, NASA and the space program had
gone through many changes. The first walk on the
moon in 1969 was followed by the first flight of
Skylab, the space station, in 1973. The first space
shuttle flight took place in 1981.

Meanwhile, Glenn remained in the Senate,
improving his political skills. Ohio voters were
familiar with Glenn and liked his moderate political
ideas. He was neither too conservative nor too
liberal. In Washington, Glenn had also become an
expert on nuclear arms control between the Soviet
Union and the United States.

Glenn also knew all about the government's day-to-day operations. His years on the Governmental Affairs Committee had made him an expert. He could talk for hours about details but still took little interest in more emotional issues such as income taxes and education. These were the issues most voters cared about. In 1984, Glenn wondered if he could be successful in a presidential election. He entered several primary elections for the Democratic presidential nomination. Many voters saw him as an honest, serious but dull politician. He did not do well early and dropped out of the race. Walter Mondale later won the

Glenn in Massachusetts, running for the Democratic presidential nomination in 1984

Democratic nomination but lost the election to Ronald Reagan.

Glenn won reelection to the Senate in 1986 with 62 percent of the vote. In the Senate, he continued to focus on military and government issues. Because of his seniority in the Senate, he was named chairman of the Governmental Affairs Committee. He helped to gain cabinet status for the Department of Veterans Affairs. This meant the head of the department was a major adviser to the president. Glenn also sponsored a law to make the Environmental Protection Agency a part of the president's cabinet. Many Republicans fought against this law.

Glenn's career had some trouble in the late 1980s. Several members of Congress had done favors for the operators of savings and loan associations, which are similar to banks. Many of these savings and loan associations ran out of money in the mid-1980s. The Department of Justice started an investigation to explain why and how this happened. In 1987, investigators learned that savings and loan directors had invested investors' money poorly. They had also paid themselves huge salaries. Charles Keating was a savings and loan operator from California. He was at the center of the investigation. Keating had once lived in Cincinnati, Ohio, and had long been a close friend of John Glenn.

In 1988, during the investigation, Glenn arranged a meeting between Keating and the

Senator Glenn *(third from the left)* talking before the Senate Ethics Commmittee in 1988

Speaker of the House, Jim Wright of Texas. As
Speaker, Wright was the most powerful member of
the House of Representatives. He could have done
important favors for Keating. Many people
suspected that Glenn had been trading political
favors for campaign money. The investigation later
cleared Glenn of this charge. Still, the Senate Ethics
Committee officially reported that Glenn had
"exercised poor judgment."

FINAL SENATE YEARS

In 1990, the Persian Gulf War started when Iraq
invaded Kuwait. President George H. W. Bush
prepared for an attack on Iraq. In early 1991, the
Senate passed the Gulf War Resolution supporting
Bush's action. Glenn was against Bush's move. He
thought the United States should not join the fight.
The United States and its allies went on to defeat
Iraq. Many of the soldiers who fought in Iraq later
suffered from illnesses caused by chemical weapons.
Glenn helped get a law passed to improve the health
benefits of these soldiers.

In 1992, Glenn was reelected with 51 percent of
the vote. The savings and loan problem had hurt his
popularity. Democrat Bill Clinton won the presidential

President Bill Clinton shakes hands with Senator Glenn after signing the Federal Acquisitions Streamlining Act of 1994.

election. For the first time in twelve years, a member of Glenn's party was in the White House.

President Bill Clinton and Vice President Al Gore had promised to make the U.S. government more efficient. Many voters thought this issue was important. Glenn helped to pass laws that cut the size of the government. The laws cut some government jobs, decreased government spending, and even reduced the amount of government paperwork.

Glenn also continued working to stop the spread of nuclear weapons. Since the 1980s, he had supported laws to prevent the sale of nuclear material to India and Pakistan. He believed these two nations in southern Asia would use the weapons against each other. Glenn made many public statements about nuclear arms. He also became a leading voice in the fight between the United States and Iraq over Iraq's attempts to build nuclear weapons.

In February 1997, Glenn announced that he would not run for a fifth Senate term. He was in

At Muskingum College with his wife Annie, Glenn announced that he will not run for reelection in 1998.

his mid-seventies. He was not as interested in Washington politics anymore. Instead, he thought about a possible return to space.

A RETURN TO SPACE

Ever since his splashdown aboard *Friendship 7*, John Glenn had hoped to return to space. He'd shared his enthusiasm with NASA leaders over the years. Glenn knew he had the ability and experience to go. Already, teachers and even congressmen had ridden the shuttle.

By 1995, Glenn had become interested in issues concerning the elderly. The number of elderly people in the country was rising. Issues such as health care, Social Security, and retirement were becoming more important. Glenn also noticed that the effects of aging were like the effects of weightlessness. He told NASA that he wanted to return to space to study those effects.

NASA thought about Glenn's request for more than a year. Finally, NASA director Daniel Goldin decided to give Glenn his chance. The good publicity of sending Glenn to space was worth the risks of him getting hurt or even dying.

On January 16, 1998, NASA made the official

announcement. John Glenn would be aboard *Discovery*. It had been thirty-six years since his last trip. But Glenn had a lot of training to do before he'd be ready. He spent time in Texas undergoing medical tests. He went through the centrifuge drill, for example. Laying on a flat bed that swings around fast, Glenn experienced 3 gs–the pressure at shuttle launch.

THE FLIGHT OF DISCOVERY

(Above) The space shuttle *Discovery* lifts off its launchpad in 1998 with John Glenn and six other astronauts aboard.

ON OCTOBER 29, 1998, *Discovery* lifted from its launchpad at Cape Canaveral, Florida, and roared into orbit. Seven astronauts were on board. They were Chiaki Mukai, Pedro Duque, Scott Parazynski, Steven Lindsey, Curtis Brown Jr., flight commander Stephen Robinson, and Senator John Glenn. *Discovery* was very different from *Friendship 7*. The ship had plenty of room for the crew, and it was much faster. Glenn would make 134 orbits instead of the 3 he had made in 1962. The orbits would cover a distance of 3.6 million miles over nine days.

Glenn's main job was to do experiments on himself. He gave a total of thirty blood samples before, during, and after the flight. Scientists measured the buildup and breakdown of proteins in his blood. Glenn also gave sixteen urine samples. He wore a special sleep-study suit that measured his brain waves, eye movement, and breathing.

Glenn measured his body temperature, blood pressure, and bone mass. He also took samples from the rest of the crew. After *Discovery* returned to Earth, these measurements were compared to measurements taken just before the flight. Changes in his body while in orbit were compared to his "normal" state on the ground.

Glenn works on an experiment inside *Discovery*.

SPACE SHUTTLE TAKEOFF AND RETURN

A space shuttle takes off by using the fuel in its solid rocket boosters and the external tank. Once the boosters are empty, they fall back to Earth by parachutes. The tank falls into the ocean. In orbit, a spacecraft's doors open to release or pick up a satellite.

An orbiter returns to Earth by firing two engines to slow down. The spacecraft enters Earth's atmosphere at a speed of more than sixteen thousand miles per hour. It then moves into landing position. It lands on a runway at a speed of about two hundred miles per hour.

Scientists studied the results for clues about the effects of spaceflight. The results will help NASA make decisions about using elderly astronauts on future missions.

The flight of *Discovery* went well. On November 7, the shuttle touched down at Cape Canaveral about 1:00 P.M. After leaving *Discovery,* Glenn said, "One g and I feel fine!" His second trip into space had been a success. But he was glad to return to Earth. He had promised Annie that it was his last flight.

A HERO'S FINISH

Glenn's shuttle trip renewed public interest in the space program. It also showed that an elderly person could take on difficult mental and physical challenges.

Not everyone was happy about Glenn's *Discovery* mission. Some writers described it as a publicity stunt. Others said it was just a senator taking a free trip without serious goals. They pointed out that several other elderly candidates had also been available. Some people thought that NASA chose Glenn because they wanted future favors from Congress.

COMPARE AND CONTRAST

	Friendship 7	Discovery
Altitude (miles)	162	325
Circuit breakers	20	961
Computers aboard	0	5
Crew space (cubic feet)	36	2,325
Distance (miles)	75,679	3,600,000
Flight time	4 hours, 56 minutes	213 hours, 44 minutes
Items aboard	48	2,600
Launch site	Cape Canaveral Air Station Cape Canaveral, Florida	Kennedy Space Center Cape Canaveral, Florida
Maximum g's	7.7	3
Orbits	3	134
Passengers	1 (male)	7 (6 males, 1 female)
Push buttons	8	219
Toggle switches	56	856
Windows	1	10
Year of flight	1962	1998

Others were happy about the flight. To many people, John Glenn was still a hero for his flight aboard *Friendship 7.* They saw his return to space at the age of seventy-seven as another act of courage.

Astronaut John Glenn waves to the cheering crowds as he and Annie ride in an open car. New York City gave them a parade on November 16, 1998.

His mission reminded many of what the nation can accomplish. "Never mind that the carpers call this mission useless," Roger Rosenblatt wrote in *Time* magazine. "The public does not require usefulness beyond its own admiring pleasure. As for the practicalities of the space program, it was never so useful as when it reminded the country of heroic capabilities."

On November 16, 1998, Glenn and Annie rode together in a parade through New York City. The scene reminded some of 1962, when Glenn and the other Mercury astronauts were given the largest ticker-tape parade in New York's history.

The parade was a joyous finish of a long career as a pilot, an astronaut, and a senator. Glenn was again playing a role that he had begun more than fifty years before. He was an American hero.

air force: a branch, or section, of the nation's armed forces. The air force is responsible for military operations in the air. Until 1947, the U.S. Army and U.S. Navy each had separate air forces. In 1947, the U.S. Air Force was created as a separate service.

Cape Canaveral: since 1961 the location in Florida from which manned spaceflights are launched. The site is officially called Cape Kennedy, after President John F. Kennedy.

centrifuge drill: a high-tech bed that whirls around for nine minutes extremely fast. People taking the drill experience the g-force as they would during a space shuttle launch.

Democratic Party: one of the two major political parties in the United States. Glenn belongs to the Democratic Party. The other major party is the Republican Party.

Distinguished Flying Cross: a military award given to a soldier for bravery or great work during a battle with airplanes

g-force: a unit of measurement that tells how much gravitational force, or g-force, is being put on a human body when it is traveling fast

gravity: the force that pulls things down toward Earth and keeps them from floating away into space

NASA: a government agency. The National Aeronautics and Space Administration was created in 1958 to coordinate flights beyond Earth's atmosphere. NASA employs thousands of scientists, engineers, and technicians. It has office complexes throughout the country.

Republican Party: one of the two major political parties in the United States. The Democratic Party, Glenn's party, is the other.

retro-rocket: a type of engine that, when turned on, helps to slow down a spacecraft so it can reenter Earth's atmosphere

rocket: a type of engine that can travel extremely fast. Rockets that launch space capsules are shaped like tubes and have a pointed end. Inside the tube are two to four stages, or sections. Each stage has its own rocket engine and fuel. The stages keep pushing the spacecraft farther into space. As the fuel in each stage is used up, the stage breaks away from the tube. The Mercury program used Atlas and Redstone rockets.

simulator: a machine that allows a person to experience what it's like to perform a certain complex task, such as flying into space. Simulators help astronauts train before they actually go on a mission.

space shuttle: a spacecraft that can bring people and cargo into space and back again

5 Kennedy Space Center, "Air-Ground Communications of the MA-6 Flight," transcript, *Mercury 7 Archives,* August 25, 2002, <http://science.ksc.nasa.gov/history/mercury/ma-6/docs/ma-6-transcript-1.html> (May 25, 2004).

34 Tom Wolfe, *The Right Stuff* (New York: Farrar, Straus and Giroux, 1979), 60.

38 Donald K. Slayton, *Deke! U.S. Manned Space: From Mercury to the Shuttle,* with Michael Cassutt (New York: Tom Doherty Associates Inc., 1994), 73.

40–41 Ibid., 74.

47 Wolfe, 180.

53 Kennedy Space Center, "Air-Ground Communications of the MA-6 Flight."

53 Peter Bond, *Heroes in Space: From Gagarin to Challenger* (New York: Basil Blackwell, 1987), 41.

55 Ibid.

57 "Retiring to Space: A Renaissance Man Aims to Retire with a Flourish," *CNN.com,* n.d., <http://www.cnn.com/SPECIALS/space/glenn/profile/> (May 25, 2004).

60 Frank Van Riper, *Glenn: The Astronaut Who Would Be President* (New York: Empire Books, 1983), 178.

80 John Glenn, *John Glenn: A Memoir,* with Nick Taylor (New York: Bantam Books, 1999), 325.

89 Ibid., 334.

95 "Senator John Glenn," *CNN.com,* July 25, 1997, <http://www.cnn.com/ALLPOLITICS/1997/gen/resources/players/glenn/> (May 25, 2004).

103 " 'I feel fine:' Glenn returns to Earth," *CNN.com,* November 7, 1998, <http://www.cnn.com/TECH/space/9811/07/shuttle.03/> (May 25, 2004).

105 Roger Rosenblatt, "A Realm Where Age Doesn't Count," *Time,* August 17, 1998.

SELECTED BIBLIOGRAPHY

Bond, Peter. *Heroes in Space: From Gagarin to Challenger.* New York: Basil Blackwell, 1987.

Cassutt, Michael. *Who's Who in Space.* Boston: G. K. Hall, 1987.

Collins, Michael. *Carrying the Fire: An Astronaut's Journey.* New York: Farrar, Straus and Giroux, 1974.

Politics in America 1998: The 105th Congress. Washington, D.C.: Congressional Quarterly Press, 1997.

Rosenblatt, Roger, "A Realm Where Age Doesn't Count," *Time,* August 17, 1998.

Slayton, Donald K. *Deke! U.S. Manned Space: From Mercury to the Shuttle.* With Michael Cassutt. New York. Tom Doherty Associates Inc., 1994.

Van Riper, Frank. *Glenn: The Astronaut Who Would Be President.* New York: Empire Books, 1983.

Wolfe, Tom. *The Right Stuff.* New York: Farrar, Straus and Giroux, 1979.

FURTHER READING AND WEBSITES

Briggs, Carol S. *Women in Space.* Minneapolis: Lerner Publications Company, 1999.

Cole, Michael D. *Friendship 7: First American in Orbit.* Berkeley Heights, NJ: Enslow, 1995.

Dartford, Mark. *Fighter Planes.* Minneapolis: Lerner Publications Company, 2004.

Donovan, Sandy. *Running for Office: A Look at Political Campaigns.* Minneapolis: Lerner Publications Company, 2004.

Feldman, Ruth Tenzer. *How Congress Works: A Look at the Legislative Branch.* Minneapolis: Lerner Publications Company, 2004.

Feldman, Ruth Tenzer. *The Korean War*. Minneapolis: Lerner Publications Company, 2004.

Holden, Henry M. *Trailblazing Astronaut John Glenn*. Berkeley Heights, NJ: Enslow, 2004.

John and Annie Glenn Historic Site and Exploration Center <http://www.johnglennhome.org> Visit the Glenn home in New Concord, Ohio.

John F. Kennedy Library and Museum–John Glenn Exhibit <http://www.jfklibrary.org/john_glenn_exhibit.html> Watch Glenn's 1962 orbit of Earth.

Kennedy, Gregory P. *The First Men in Space*. Broomhall, PA: Chelsea House, 1991.

Kennedy Space Center–Project Mercury <http://science.ksc.nasa.gov/history/mercury/> The home page of the Mercury program gives all the details of each Mercury mission and the astronauts who participated in them.

Kupperberg, Paul. *John Glenn: The First American in Orbit and His Return to Space*. New York: Rosen Publishing, 2004.

Maynard, Chris. *Aircraft*. Minneapolis: LernerSports, 1999.

McPherson, Stephanie Sammartino, and Joseph Sammartino Gardner. *Wilber & Orville Wright: Taking Flight*. Minneapolis: Carolrhoda Books, Inc., 2004.

O'Brien, Patrick. *Fantastic Flights: One Hundred Years of Flying on the Edge*. New York: Walker & Co., 2003.

Sherman, Josepha. *The Cold War*. Minneapolis: Lerner Publications Company, 2004.

Somervill, Barbara A. *The History of Space Travel*. Chanhassen, MN: Child's World, 2004.

PHOTO ACKNOWLEDGMENTS

Photographs are used with the permission of: National Aeronautic and Space Administration (NASA), pp. 4, 30, 51, 52, 54, 59, 61, 100, 101; © Bettmann/CORBIS, pp. 6, 8, 18, 27, 28, 49, 56, 72 (both), 73, 83, 89, 92, 94; Classmates.com Yearbook Archives, pp. 10, 11 (both); United States Holocaust Memorial Museum, p. 12; Library of Congress, p. 13; National Archives W&C #733, p. 16; U.S. Airforce Museum, p. 22; National Museum of Aviation, p. 24; AP/Wide World Photos, pp. 29, 40, 41, 44, 67, 77, 79, 81, 86, 96, 97; © Lambert/ Getty Images, p. 43; © H. Allen/Getty Images, p. 46; The John F. Kennedy Library, pp. 63, 64; National Archives, pp. 70, 71, 76; © Hulton|Archive by Getty Images, pp. 80, 90; © Timothy A. Clary/ AFP/Getty Images, p. 105.

Cover image by National Aeronautic and Space Administration (NASA).